*Applied
Theosophy*

By Henry S. Olcott

Copyright © 2021 Lamp of Trismegistus. All rights reserved. No part of this publication may be reproduced or transmitted in any form or by any means, electronic or mechanical, including photocopying, recording, or by any information storage and retrieval system, without permission in writing from Lamp of Trismegistus. Reviewers may quote brief passages.

ISBN: 978-1-63118-592-2

Esoteric Classics

Other Books in this Series and Related Titles

The Hymns of Hermes by G R S Mead (978-1-63118-405-5)

Clairvoyance and Psychic Abilities by A Besant &c (978-1-63118-403-1)

Gnosis of the Mind by G R S Mead (978-1-63118-408-6)

Freemasonry and the Egyptian Mysteries by C. W. Leadbeater (978-1-63118-456-7)

Dreams: What They Are and Caused by C W Leadbeater (978–1–63118–570–0)

An Outline of Theosophy by C W Leadbeater (978-1-63118-452-9)

Paracelsus, the Four Elements and Their Spirits by M P Hall (978-1-63118-400-0)

Essays on Ancient Magic by Helena P Blavatsky (978-1-63118-535-9)

Essays on the Esoteric Tradition of Karma by A Besant &c (978-1-63118-426-0)

The Use of Evil by Annie Besant (978-1-63118-532-8)

Occult Arts by William Q. Judge (978-1-63118-559-5)

The Alchemical Catechism of Paracelsus by Paracelsus (978-1-63118-513-7)

Alchemy in the Nineteenth Century by Helena P Blavatsky (978-1-63118-446-8)

Qabbalistic Teachings and the Tree of Life by M P Hall (978-1-63118-482-6)

The Historic, Mythic and Mystic Christ by Annie Besant (978–1–63118–533–5)

The Hidden Mysteries of Christianity by Annie Besant (978–1–63118–534–2)

The Brotherhood of Religions by Annie Besant (978–1–63118–563–2)

The Religion of Theosophy by Bhagwan Das (978–1–63118–565–6)

Arcane Formulas or Mental Alchemy by W W Atkinson (978-1-63118-459-8)

The Machinery of the Mind by Dion Fortune (978-1-63118-451-2)

The Leadbeater Reader: A Selection of Occult Essays (978-1-63118-483-3)

Audio versions are also available on Audible, Amazon and Apple

Other Books in this Series and Related Titles

Higher Consciousness by C W Leadbeater (978–1–63118–591–5)

Theories About Reincarnation and Spirits by H P Blavatsky (978–1–63118–590–8)

The Use and Power of Thought by C W Leadbeater (978–1–63118–589–2)

Commentary on the Pymander by G R S Mead (978–1–63118–588–5)

Hypnotism and Mesmerism by Annie Besant (978–1–63118–587–8)

Spirits of Various Kinds by Helena P Blavatsky (978–1–63118–586–1)

The Hidden Language of Symbolism by Annie Besant (978–1–63118–585–4)

Eastern Magic & Western Spiritualism by Henry S Olcott (978–1–63118–584–7)

Spiritual Progress and Practical Occultism by H P Blavatsky (978–1–63118–583–0)

Memory and Consciousness by Besant & Blavatsky (978–1–63118–582–3)

The Origin of Evil by Helena P Blavatsky (978–1–63118–581–6)

The Camp of Philosophy: Studies in Alchemy by Bloomfield (978–1–63118–580–9)

The Testaments of the Twelve Patriarchs (978–1–63118–579–3)

Occult or Exact Science? by Helena P Blavatsky (978–1–63118–578–6)

Occultism, Semi-Occultism & Pseudo Occultism by A Besant (978–1–63118–577–9)

The Fourth-Gospel and Synoptical Problem by G R S Mead (978–1–63118–576–2)

On the Bhagavad-Gita by T Subba Row &c (978–1–63118–575–5)

What Theosophy Does for Us by C W Leadbeater (978–1–63118–574–8)

Spiritual Life for Man by Annie Besant (978–1–63118–573–1)

The Mysteries by Annie Besant (978–1–63118–572–4)

Fundamental Ideas of Theosophy by Bhagwan Das (978–1–63118–571–7)

Audio versions are also available on Audible, Amazon and Apple

Table of Contents

Introduction...7

Applied Theosophy
By Henry S. Olcott...9

How Best to Become a Theosophist
By Henry S. Olcott...25

How Best to Become a Theosophist
By George Wyld...29

Notes on the Above
By Henry S. Olcott...31

Theosophy and its Opponents
By Henry S. Olcott...35

INTRODUCTION

The word "esoteric" can be difficult to define. Esotericism in general can be seen less as a system of beliefs and more as a category, which encompasses numerous, different systems of beliefs. It's a bit of juxtaposition, since the word "esoteric" indicates something that few people know about, while the term itself broadly covers numerous philosophies, practices, areas of study and belief systems.

In a greater sense, Esotericism acts as a storehouse for secret knowledge, which is often considered ancient (by *tradition, if not by fact)*, passed down from generation to generation, in private. At various times in history, simply possessing the knowledge of some of these subjects, was considered illegal and a jailable offence, if discovered. This usually included such general topics as Alchemy, Pharmacology, Qabalah, Hermeticism, Occultism, Ceremonial Magic, Astrology, Divination, Rosicrucianism and so on. Collectively, these areas of study were often referred to as the esoteric sciences.

Sometimes, the outer garment of a subject isn't esoteric, while what is hidden beneath it, is. As an example, Freemasonry isn't necessarily esoteric by nature (at *least not anymore)*, but certain signs, passwords and handshakes given to the candidate during their initiation, are in fact, esoteric, in the sense that they are hidden from the general public.

Today, in the twenty-first century, such topics are readily available at bookstores across the country, and numerous mainsteam publishers offer beginners guides and coffee-table volumes on many of these subjects, intended for mass appeal. Books like "*The Secret*" have turned previously arcane topics into household knowledge. All that being the case, however, it isn't to say that there still aren't buried secrets to uncover, ancient wisdom being ignored and forgotten mysteries to be explored. In fact, it is often that we are only able to further our own studies by standing on the shoulders of these disappearing giants.

Lamp of Trismegistus is doing its part to help preserve humanity's esoteric history by making some of these classics available to those students who are seeking to unearth the knowledge of these ancient colossi.

So, be sure to check other titles from our *Esoteric Classics* series, as well as our *Occult Fiction, Theosophical Classics, Foundations of Freemasonry Series, Supernatural Fiction, Paranormal Research Series, Studies in Buddhism* and our *Christian Apocrypha Series*. You can also download the audio versions of most of these titles from Amazon, Apple or Audible, for learning on the go.

APPLIED THEOSOPHY
by H.S. Olcott

People speak of pure mathematics and applied mathematics; the former belong properly to the region of the ideal, not of the ideal in the sense of the fanciful, for there is nothing less fanciful than mathematics, but the ideal in the sense of the metaphysical, which is the really real; the latter is the very imperfect expression of the former in terms of matter, and roughly utilized for the purposes of this mundane existence. Now it is a question which demands the very serious attention of the Fellows of this Society, whether there does not exist something which bears the same relation to "pure Theosophy" that applied mathematics bear to pure. If "applied Theosophy" expresses any real idea, what is implied in the term? Can the Fellows of the Theosophical Society apply their knowledge to the affairs of our mundane existence? Is it possible to materialize, however imperfectly, the great mass of high aspirations and altruistic sentiments that have accumulated in the literature of Theosophy and in the souls of Theosophists, and which at present, for want of an outlet, seem to threaten us with a congestion of spirituality?

The first question that naturally arises is, whether the action of the Theosophical Society in every respect should be limited to its declared Objects. On the general principle that every one should mind his own business, the presumption is in favor of this view. No one on joining our Society relinquishes his right to take a personal part in any other movement for the benefit of his fellow men, nor escapes his duty of doing so. But every "Cause" has its special organization and organs, and pre-empted field of work, and if the Objects of the Theosophical Society are taken seriously by its Fellows, are they not enough to occupy very fully all the time and energy these are likely to be able to spare from the routine business of life? Of the three Objects, two are distinctly separated from everything else. The study of Eastern philosophies, religions and sciences, and the investigation of the obscure forces in Nature and powers in man, are specialties, which have little or no direct connection with the altruism which it is the peculiar function of Theosophy as an ethical system to publish to the world; more than this, they may be said to be both of them unsocial in their nature, since their tendency is to isolate anyone who seriously occupies himself with them from sympathetic intercourse with his neighbors. The first Object is altogether different. To "form the nucleus of Universal Brotherhood," so far from conducing to retirement and concentration, is a purpose so high, so deep, so broad, so universally sympathetic, so distant of realization, that it becomes vague and confused when the attention is directed to it, and to most Fellows this Object is about equivalent in practice to the formation of a nucleus for the recurrence of the Golden Age, or for the re-establishment of the Garden of Eden.

Now, experience proves, what reason might have foreseen, that a comparatively small proportion of the Fellows of the Society take up seriously either of the two *contracting* Objects, and that only an exceptionally enthusiastic Brother is *moved to action* by the *expanding* one; from which it follows that as far as concerns any activity or good influence in the *practical* affairs of life, the Fellows as a corporate body might as well be shut up in a little community like the Shakers, from whom the world hears once in every ten years or so.

If this, however, were all there were in the Theosophical Society, it would never have become the well- known, by many much esteemed, and, in certain quarters, roundly abused, institution that it is. The fact is that those who join the Society bring into it their knowledge and their activity, and the reputation of the Society has been built up by the individual efforts of its Fellows. Take away *Isis Unveiled; The Secret Doctrine; Light on the Path; Esoteric Buddhism; Theosophy, Religion, and the Occult Science,* and half a dozen other works, together with Theosophical magazines -- all of them distinctly due to personal effort — and what would be left of the renown or notoriety of the Society? Since, however, the Theosophical Society is composed of its Fellows, and is what its Fellows make it, to say all that is in no way to disparage the Society, any more than it would detract from the beauty or utility of a Coral Island in the South Seas, to say that it owed its existence to the individual labors of the little lives that raised it from the bottom of the ocean. It is a mass of coral cells certainly, but it is something more it is a coral Island, with an added individuality of its own.

What the Society has hitherto done — its great merit in the eyes of some, and its terrible fault in the estimation of others — is *to make people think.* No one can for long belong to the Theosophical Society without beginning to question *himself.* He begins to ask himself: "How do I know that?". "Why do I believe this?" "What reason have I to be so certain that I am right, and so sure that my neighbors are wrong?" "What is my warrant for declaring this action, or that practice, to be good, and their opposite bad?" The very air of Theosophy is charged with the spirit of enquiry. It is not the "skeptical" spirit, nor is it the "agnostic". It is a real desire to know and to learn the truth, as far as it is possible for any creature to know it who is so limited by his capacities and so biased by his prejudices as is man. It is *that* which has raised the Theosophical Society above the level of all other aggregations or organizations of men, and which, so long as its Fellows abstain from dogmatizing, must keep it on an altogether higher plane. To the Theologian, to the Philosopher, to the Skeptic, to the Spiritualist, to the Materialist, it says the same thing — study man and Nature, and compare what you find there with your own pre-existing ideas and theories. In proportion as anyone follows this advice he spontaneously inclines towards Theosophy, which is the least common multiple and greatest common measure of all the "ists," the "tys" and the "isms". There is nothing in the Objects of the Society which would enable any person unacquainted with its history to divine from them alone what would be the ideas of a Fellow of the Society upon almost any subject. The fact is that the Theosophical Society attracts persons who have got a natural disposition to examine, analyze, reflect; and when this tendency does not exist — when people join the Society from special sympathy with one or more of its Objects — they very soon begin to ponder over the problems of existence, for they find themselves involuntarily and instinctively subjecting their own pet theories and cherished weaknesses to the process of examination which is the slogan of the Society. The result of an examination thus candidly made is almost invariably a view of life and of the universe in more or less resemblance to that of the Eastern religions and philosophies when these are purified of their superstition and priest-made masks. It is a mistake to imagine that what is known as Theosophy at present has been learned from the writings of the ancients; it is *an* independent growth in the modern mind which to many appears spontaneous, because they cannot discern whence the seeds come. Theosophy, like man himself, has many different sources. All Science, all Philosophy, all Religion, are its progenitors; it appears when the seed of an enquiring spirit is dropped into a personal soil sufficiently unprejudiced and altruistic to give it nourishment. The modern world is thinking out the problems of life in the rough, and then comparing its conclusions with the ideas of the ancients by way of corroborating or verifying them. Here and there a Fellow of the Society outside of India may be found who is willing to accept the Eastern Initiates, whether ancient or modern, as teachers; but the majority prefer to think and theorize for themselves, which is, after all, the best way for anyone to learn who can think and theorize logically.

We have, then, a Society without opinions, but with certain "Objects", certain principles, and certain methods, and we have as a result a tendency to certain modes of thought, and certain theories of the Universe, to which theories the name of Theosophy has been given, and when these theories are examined, they are found not only to resemble those contained in the Eastern systems of philosophy, but a closer scrutiny shows that the very same ideas, only sadly mutilated, underlie all religions, and are contained in a more or less diluted form in all philosophies. Not only this: a careful comparison of the root of the Theosophical system with the latest discoveries and most advanced conjectures of modern science, and of recent experimental research in the borderland between physics and metaphysics shows an extraordinary agreement between them. We are advancing step by step; a student can take in at a time from a teacher only a very small addition to the knowledge which he already possesses, and the fact that *The Secret Doctrine* has been so generally understood and so highly appreciated by Theosophists, shows that their own thoughts were not so very much behind the ideas *given out* in that marvelous work.

All this, however, is only what may be called the intellectual or philosophical side of Theosophy; and it is the fruit of the Theosophical Society's influence only in one direction. Those who come under the influence of the Theosophic spirit are affected ethically as well as philosophically. The same causes which produce a certain tendency in *thought* produce also a disposition to *act* in a certain manner. The habit of viewing the Universe and men's lives as a divinely wonderful system, in which progress towards ultimate perfection by means of conscious effort is the furthest analysis which we can make of the purpose of existence, results in a desire to exert the necessary effort in order to ensure for ourselves, and for those whom we can help, as much of that progress as is realizable at present. It is impossible for anyone seriously to believe that this world is governed by a law of absolute justice — that as we sow, so shall we reap — without finding his ideas of the value of life, and of the things of life, radically affected thereby. If it be in our power to become larger and stronger beings, richer in ourselves and happier in our lives, no one but a fool would refuse to avail himself of the means of attaining to that happier and higher state. If it be possible to help others to reach it, no one but a selfish and unsympathetic wretch would refuse to his neighbor the helping hand for which he feels he would himself be grateful. The consequence is that along with enlargement of the mind there takes place an enlargement of the sympathies as the result of Theosophic studies, and both of these conduce to the moral growth of the individual. This moral growth exhibits itself in two ways, internally and externally. The individual in whom it takes place begins to regulate and purify his own life; he casts away from him all that he feels will keep him weak and silly, and cultivates those habits and those qualities that he knows will make him strong. He also tried to induce his neighbors to enter the upward path, and endeavors to help those who show a disposition to turn away from the harmful and the idiotic, which form so large a proportion of the affairs of men's lives at present. The help he can be to single individuals is comparatively small; for the work they, like himself, have to do at first is the rectifying of their own faults and the purifying of their own motives, and this every man must necessarily do for himself; and a neighbor, however anxious to assist, can do but little more than exhort and encourage him. But over and above these personal faults and evils, there are others which affect a great number of persons together, against which any single individual is powerless. Even were the dislike and fear of those wider evils general, and every one agreed that they ought to be put down, still unless a united attack be made upon them they cannot be abated, for individuals can make no impression on them, and they are strong enough to resist the attack of a mob. To combat them requires unanimity and organization. Every Fellow of the Society feels in his heart a strong wish to aid to the best of his ability in diminishing and if possible, destroying these evils. He sees that their existence is completely incompatible with any success in establishing a nucleus of Universal Brotherhood. He knows that they have their root deep down in human selfishness, and that they are supported by many existing institutions, political, social and religious — to which they are firmly attached by established customs and vested interests.

Now it is at that point that the hitch occurs. The Theosophical Society is not supposed to promulgate opinions concerning social matters, any more than it is supposed to do so concerning religious matters; and as for politics, they are strictly prohibited to the Fellows, as Fellows, by the Constitution and Rules of the Society, although *personally* they may and often do take an active interest therein. Again, if anyone proposes that the Theosophical Society shall take any part in the war against the practical evils of life, it is answered that, as has been previously said, each evil has already got a special organization to oppose it. There are special Societies for the suppression of drunkenness, of cruelty, of immorality in various forms; also for the furtherance of every kind of benevolent work; were the Theosophical Society therefore to interest itself in these things, not only would it be going out of its legitimate province, but it would be an interloper in the fields which others have got a prescriptive right to occupy. Now this would be a serious argument, but for one very obvious consideration; namely, that since the

Theosophical Society has professedly, as a body, no opinion on any subject, it is equally a transgression of its basic principles for it to sustain or promulgate any special system of philosophy, as in practice it decidedly does, under the name of "Theosophy". The Theosophical Society may be, and nominally is, a Society for the stimulation of enquiry and research, overshadowed by the somewhat vague idea of the ultimate realization of human brotherhood; but we have seen already that those who enter the Society either possess already or very soon acquire, certain definite habits of mind and ways of viewing the Universe, which are denoted and connoted by the terms Theosophy and Theosophist. Now it is distinctly as a result of these ideas and habits that there arises a desire, not indeed peculiar to Theosophists, but inseparable from Theosophy, to rid the world of evil practices and evil forces; and it follows logically that the desire to act rightly is as much a consequence of a connection with Theosophy as the desire to think rightly; and that therefore both are natural, spontaneous, and inevitable consequences of Fellowship in the Theosophical Society and equally within the legitimate sphere of the Society, whether manifested individually, or by the united effort of a part, or of the whole of the Fellows. A Theosophist is necessarily imbued with what was called in the Middle Ages, and is called to this day by those who are still in the mediaeval condition of mind, a hatred of Satan and all his works. To combat evil actively is, in fact, the ungratified desire at present of thousands of Fellows of the Society, and it is chiefly because there is now no outlet for their activity in that direction, which takes their attention off of themselves and away from each other, that quarrels and scandals occur among its Fellows. Only a small percentage of the Fellows care very much to work at Occultism, and now there is a separate division of the Society set apart for that purpose, under a Teacher eminently qualified to teach *real* Occultism if she only had pupils capable of learning it.

This, then, is the problem, and it is of all the problems presented to us at the present moment that which is of most importance to the Theosophical Society: Having prepared themselves by study and self- development to take an active part in the warfare against evil, can any means be devised whereby the Fellows of the Society can apply their knowledge and their energies to the practical affairs of life? *Practical Theosophy* is an affair of the future. *Applied Theosophy* is a more modest ambition, and is, or ought to be, a possibility.

Now it is evident that no greater mistake could be made than to open little departments in the Society itself for different special purposes. A Temperance division, Social purity division, a Woman's rights division, an Anti-cruelty division, would be so many mistakes, unless the intention were similar to that which was manifested in the establishment of the Esoteric Division — to isolate a certain group of Fellows from the main work of the Society, for the mutual benefit of all concerned. It would be a blunder, not only because these special divisions would intrude upon the work now being done by special organizations, but also because the *real work of the Theosophical Society is, and always must be, accomplished upon the plane of ideas, not on that of material things.* Moreover any specialization of functions tends not only to develop a particular part, but also to draw into that part all that appertains to the exercise of that function, previously contained in the other parts. Already the effect of clearly divided Objects has been the formation in the Society of unrecognized but not unreal divisions, in the shape of groups which are exclusively addicted to psychic experiments, to the philosophy of the Hindus, to ethics of Buddhism, or to the speculations of modern Western thinkers. Were the Fellows encouraged to follow their natural affinities in the application of their Theosophy to the affairs of life, as they do their predilections for the study of Theosophy in one or other of its various aspects, they would become still more one-sided and partially developed Theosophists than they are at present, and this further isolation of its Fellows from one another would tend to weaken the Society still more as a united body.

If the Fellows of the Theosophical Society are to apply their Theosophy to the affairs of life, it must be through the Society, and as individual units of the whole — not as isolated individuals. It is well known that in metaphysics two and two do not make four but five, and that the fifth is frequently by far the most important part of the sum. The same idea is expressed in the fable of the bundle of sticks; tied together they are unbreakable, singly they can be snapped with ease. Union or unity adds certain qualities and powers that were not there before, and the vehicle in which these powers reside is the unit which is added to the number of the sticks by tying them together. It is this mystic individuality, "the sum total"; that gives strength to all societies and congregations of men, and becomes the real dominating power, to which all contribute some of their force and which stands behind every unit and lends its whole strength to it. Without it a Fellow of the Theosophical Society would be as powerless as any other isolated man or woman in the community. With it behind him an F.T.S is a power in proportion to the unity and singleness of purpose of the Society to which he belongs. Who speaks when a priest of the Roman Catholic Church utters a command? *The united power of the Church of Rome.* Who speaks when a disfrocked priest says something? *A nonentity.* Who speaks when the Judge, the General, the Statesman open their mouths? " The State — the tremendous and often tyrannical personality that comes into life and action when the units that composed it are bound together, through organization, by a common will and a common purpose.

It is this added increment, and this only, that gives to the Theosophical Society its extraordinary, and to many unaccountable, power. Weak in numbers, contemptible in organization, distracted by personal jealousies, subject to constant endeavors on the part of ambitious individuals to break it up into pieces which they can distribute among themselves, the Theosophical Society is a power in the world notwithstanding all the assaults that are made upon it by outsiders, and the disintegrating influences within. Why? Because upon a plane higher than the physical the Fellows are united and strong. They are united in their ideas of the purpose of life, and of the government of the Universe — in other words, they are strong in that they are individual cells composing the body called the Theosophical Society, as it exists in both the physical and the spiritual worlds.

Quarrel as they may among themselves, be as small and provincial as they choose, the Fellows of the Society cannot help contributing their little quota of Theosophical ideas to that united whole idea which is the spirit of the Theosophical Society, and therefore its very life and real self. And those who attack the Society are frequently its supporters; for they attack it on the external plane, while, unknown to themselves in spite of themselves, they support it upon the plane where its real life is passed, for those who are its enemies are generally ignorant of its true nature, and are frequently themselves imbued with eminently Theosophic ideas and aspirations, which nourish the Society on the ideal plane, and constantly tend to draw those in whom they exist, more and more in the direction of the Theosophical Society in its materialized form on earth.

If then the real power of Theosophy in the world is exercised in the realm of thought; and if the direction in which that power is exerted is a natural consequence of the growth of certain ideas in the minds of those who carry out the objects of the Society, it stands to reason that the gigantic evils of our modern world must be attacked with immaterial weapons and in the intellectual and moral planes. How can this be accomplished? Simply by perceiving the fact, understanding it and acknowledging it. Then the actual work will be accomplished quietly, almost silently, and apparently spontaneously, just as the great reforming work of the Society is now being accomplished — by individuals — who, while contributing to the strength of the Society, draw from it in return a force that gives to their utterances an importance and a power which had they spoken as isolated individuals, and not as Fellows of the Society, their words would not have had.

There does not, and can not, exist the slightest doubt as to the direction in which the power of the Theosophical Society would be applied in practical things. If the tendency of Fellowship in the Society is to develop certain habits of philosophic thought, its tendency is even stronger to give rise to definite ethical views and moral principles. However much and bitterly the Fellows may disagree as to the duration of Devachan or the number and viability of the Principles in man, or any other point of occult doctrine, it would be hard to get up a dispute among the brethren as to the evil of intemperance, or the abomination of cruelty, or about any other of the crying sins of our times. Not only is that the case but they would all give the same reasons, for their detestation of these evils, reasons founded on their Theosophical ideas and principles. Still, of what avail or utility to the world are their ideas and wishes in these matters at present? Who cares to have the good-word or influence of the Theosophical Society for any benevolent movement, any reform, or any attempt to do justice? *No One*. There is not a "cause" today that would not rather see the minister of some microscopic Christian sect on the platform at its Annual Meeting than the most prominent member of the Theosophical Society — for the good and sufficient reason that the Rev Gentleman would carry with him the unseen but not unfelt influence and authority of the body to which he belongs, while the F.T.S would represent nothing but himself. This condition of things should not exist, and all that is needed to remedy it is for all of us to see and understand that *the ethical* is just as much a part of the Theosophical idea, and just as much the business of the Fellows of the Society as *the philosophical*.

But it is only as a united whole that the Theosophical Society can ever be a power in the world for good, or a vehicle for the exercise of the altruistic efforts of its Fellows. The action of the Theosophical Society is on the plane of ideas, which is the plane of realities, in that material things are but pre-existing ideals brought down into this earthly sphere. The Theosophical Society does not mean a number of little coteries, nor a few larger coteries composed of a collection of the smaller ones. It does not mean a few hundred Presidents of little Branches, or half a score of "General Secretaries", it does not mean even the Fellows that compose the Society at any particular time, for these come and go and the Society remains intact, as the cells of the body change, while the body remains the same person, animated by the same spirit. The real Theosophical Society is an indivisible unit, animated by an individual life! Its soul is the love of truth, its vital principle is kindness, and it dwells in a world above the material, where no enemy can touch it. It depends for its manifestation on earth upon an appropriate vehicle, and the first condition necessary in that vehicle is that it shall be a *united whole*. The Theosophical Society is an ideal power for good diffused over the whole world, but it requires material conditions, and the most important of these is a material center, from which and to which the efferent and afferent forces shall circulate. This is a condition of the life of all organizations, and of all organisms, and the Theosophical Society is both; it is an organization on the material plane, an organism on the spiritual. A common center, therefore, is as necessary for spiritual as for physical reasons. "Adyar" is not a place only, it is a principle. It is a name which ought to carry with it a power far greater than that conveyed by the name "Rome". ADYAR is the center of the Theosophical movement — not "7 Duke Street, Adelphi," or "Post Office Box 2659, New York.

ADYAR is a principle and a symbol, as well as a locality. ADYAR is the name which means on the material plane the Headquarters of an international, or, more properly speaking, world-wide Society of persons who have common aims and objects, and are imbued with a common spirit. It means on the supra- physical plane a center of life and energy, the point to and from which the currents run between the ideal and the material. Every loyal Fellow has in his heart a little ADYAR, for he has in him a spark of the spiritual fire which the name typifies. ADYAR is the symbol of our unity as a Society, and so long as it exists in the heart of its Fellows the powers of the enemy can never prevail against the Theosophical Society.

What then, to recapitulate, must be our answer to the questions with which we started: Is such a thing as "Applied Theosophy" possible? If so, of what does it consist?

We have seen that there is no reason why the ideas and influence of the Theosophical Society should not be as great in combating wickedness in the practical department of life as in combating error in the philosophical. The Objects of the Society neither order nor forbid interference with either; but they predispose the Fellows to exert an active influence in both, by evolving in their minds a perception of truer and better things, and a desire for their realization. We have seen that it is not by making the Society itself an instrument on the physical plane that its power can be utilized for good; but that its influence must be a moral one, consisting of the combined and united thoughts and wishes of the whole Society, focused upon any individual point, and acting through the personality of its individual Fellows. We have seen that all that is necessary to make such a united power manifest is that its existence should be acknowledged and felt by the Fellows themselves; and that to acknowledge and feel it, and thus bring it from the latent to the active condition, the Fellows must perceive that the Theosophical Society is a living entity, "ideal" if one chooses to call it so, but an entity *one and indivisible* alike upon the material plane and on the supra-physical plane. We have also seen that the visible center of the Society, "ADYAR", is symbolical of the principle of unity, as well as of the material life of the Society, and that in every sense loyalty to "ADYAR" means loyalty to the Objects of the Society and to the principles of Theosophy.

The answer to our questions then must be that Applied Theosophy is surely a possibility; and that it consists of the moral influence brought to bear upon the practical evils of life by the exertions of individual Fellows who have behind them, severally and collectively, the spiritual power created by unity of purpose, of ideas and loyalty to the truth; a power for good of which the terrestrial ADYAR is the physical center and Headquarters; while the spiritual ADYAR is the channel by means of which powerful influences from a higher sphere, unseen but not unfelt, enter the Society through the hearts of each and all of its Fellows, thence to be outpoured upon the whole world.

HOW BEST TO BECOME A THEOSOPHIST
By Henry S. Olcott

The London *Spiritualist* gives space to a full report of the inaugural address of George Wyld, Esq., M. D., (Edin.), the newly elected President of the British Theosophical Society, a branch of our own — which we lack the room to print. Dr. Wyld's paper is marked, by the force, learning and sincerity, which are his recognized personal characteristics. It teaches the true doctrine that adeptship, or the attainment of a full spiritual condition, is only possible for those who bring the bodily lusts of all kinds under the control of the higher and better nature, and, in a series of apt quotations from the four Gospels of the New Testament, he endeavours to convince his audience that Jesus, though perhaps not the very and only Son of God, was at least the highest type of human spirituality ever vouchsafed. to mankind. At the same time. Dr. Wyld affirms that every man may become a "Son of God", his rule being *"So to empty our souls of self that the Father, becoming manifest in His Sons, illuminates and regenerates the world."* This species of Christian adeptship our respected brother places even above the adeptship of the East, which, he says "is secret and mysterious, and bidden from all except a select few, who have passed through an ordeal so severe and dangerous that many, it is said, perish in body or in soul on making the attempt, and into which select few, so far as we know, no woman has ever been admitted."

In these utterances, so foreign to the views entertained by a large majority of Theosophists, our Oriental friends will see a practical evidence of the truly republican and cosmopolitan nature of the Theosophical Society. Dr. Wyld is an enthusiastic admirer of the character of Jesus, and yet sees his way clear to the accomplishment of that personal spiritual unfolding towards which we all aspire. Indeed, it is but natural with strong thinkers, his path seems to him the best and. surest one, and he lays his scheme before his Society and the world with an ardent longing for its acceptance. Brahmos will doubtless recognize the very essence of their own ideas coming from this good Theosophist's lips, and. see that our journal was not wide of the mark in saying upon its first appearance that there was ample room for Brahmo and Prarthana Samajists and even liberal Christians, in our fellowship. Our London brother means every word he speaks on this theme, and his opinions are respected by us just as much as though he had avowed his faith in either of the ancient Eastern religions, which some of us think the best ever evolved by man. If he had been in India, studied the ancient philosophies, and seen the Eastern adepts and the practical proofs of their lofty science, he would, beyond doubt change the views he now expounds so eloquently. And all this may come in time.

But, in thus conceding to Dr. Wyld the full right of private judgment, it must not be forgotten that like the rest of us, he speaks only for himself, and neither the Theosophical Society as a whole, nor even the British branch, as a body, is responsible. The very idea of "Brotherhood of Humanity" and "Republic of Conscience," both of which synonyms apply to the basis on which our Society is building up, covers the principle of strict intellectual reciprocity, Any attempt to make the Society a propaganda, whether of Christianity or any other single religion, would at once strip it of the first quality of cosmopolitanism and make it only a sect. For myself, I am free to say that there is no adequate proof to my mind either that Jesus was the Son of God, that he said or did the things ascribed to him, that either one of the four Gospels is anything better than a literary fabrication, or that Jesus ever lived. Nor do I see that the ideal character of Jesus is any nobler than that of Gautama, if so noble.

At the proper times and places I have maintained these views, and hope to do so often again. So far from sharing Dr. Wyld's ideal of Christianity, I have, after nearly fifty years of practical observation and experience in Christian countries and among the teachers and professors of Christianity, been forced to conclude that it is a bad religion and fosters every sin and vice against which its ethical code inveighs. And yet this is but my individual opinion, and in expressing it, I no more compromise our Society than does Dr. Wyld, who is so strong an admirer of Jesus, by expressing his, or than Mr. Massey by his article in this number of the THEOSOPHIST, or the Swami Dayanand, or our orthodox Hindu fellows, or the high priest Sumangala, or any other adherent of any special sect or theology, by what they respectively teach. We are all individual and free as to personal beliefs, but are knitted together by the strong ties of intellectual reciprocity and. universal brotherhood.

Nor is Dr. Wyld warranted in his definition of the nature of Oriental adeptship, as given in the following terms: "The Oriental adept obtains magical or soul power over matter, *which he uses for his own ends* — and over spirits. But the Christian adept has no dealings with low or weak spirits, except to convert them or to cast them out, but his life is spent in openly transmuting his spiritual powers into good works for the good of mankind." The implication here is most unequivocal — the Eastern adept uses his acquired power for selfish ends and consorts with low and weak spirits with a less commendable object than that of converting or casting them out; and, unlike his Christian compeer, does not "transmute his spiritual powers into good works lor the good of mankind". Since I, as an individual, am commenting upon the opinions of Dr. Wyld as an individual, I am bound to say that nothing could be farther from the real state of the case. Whatever the Christian adept may or may not do of beneficent deeds — and church history is not all one-sided on that question — it is most certain that the Eastern adept's first and last aspiration is to benefit mankind by making himself purer and better than they. So far from consorting with low and weak spirits, the very elementary instruction he receives is to avoid them and rid himself of their fatal influence by becoming too holy for them to approach him. Not a single "Eastern adept" comes within Dr. Wyld's hypothesis, except the problematical practitioner of Black Magic or Sorcery, who uses his knowledge of arcane natural powers to gratify carnal appetites and desires, and *invariably falls victim to the evil spirits he has drawn to his aid.*

It is equally incorrect to say that no woman has become an adept. Not to mention one example which will immediately recall itself to every Theosophist, I may say that I personally have encountered in India two other initiated women, and know of a number of others in the East. Some women, it must be remembered, are of that sex only in body — taking sex to mean that negative quality of individuality which Dr. Wyld evidently had in mind when thinking of them. If Jesus made adepts by breathing on men, so that they could under this *afflatus* do "miracles"; and if Loyola, Theresa, Savonarola, and the Curé D'Ars, possessed the power of aethrobacy and healing, so have hundreds of "Eastern adepts" in Indian history healed their multitudes, "miraculously" fed the hungry, and raised the dead: as for air-walking, the readers of this paper need not be told that in India, even an English doctor admits, it is an exact physiological science.

My friend Dr. Wyld deplores that in Great Britain there are no examples of adeptship to refer to; to which I reply that I could name to him at least one British Fellow of the Society, who, in modest privacy has by intelligent self-discipline already acquired very marked results in this direction; while I have, with my own eyes, seen in the streets of London one of the most eminent of Eastern adepts, who has that to look after, which is a transmutation of his powers for the good of humanity. These "adepts", "Rosicrucians", "initiates", or whatever else we may choose to call them, go about the world — as Professor Alexander Wilder so clearly told us last month — without being suspected; mingling in crowds but not affected by them and doing what is best to be done, and out of purest love for their fellow-men. Those only are permitted to recognise them whom it is necessary they should reveal themselves to, for the attainment of a definite object. But this one thing is indisputable, that, whether they outwardly call themselves Buddhists, Hindus, Parsis or Christians, they are absolutely at one in spirit, and that spirit is to become spiritually great, so that great good may be done by them to the whole world.

How Best to Become a Theosophist

by Dr. George Wyld,
President of British Theosophical Society.
London, 19th March, 1880.

DEAR COLONEL OLCOTT,

The Theosophist for March has just come to hand, and in order to catch the post, I sit down to write to you at once a few hurried lines.

I thank you for the kind and flattering words you use in speaking of my Presidential address, but at the same time I think you somewhat fail to appreciate the fall meaning of the position I take.

When I speak of an Oriental adept, I distinctly declare that I do so with all deference, confessing my imperfect information and even my ignorance. When, for instance, I say that "the adept obtains magical powers which he uses for his own ends and over spirits", you misinterpret me by implying selfish ends and consorting with spirits.

This is the reverse of what I meant. I meant that his ends were more private than public, and that he *commanded* but did not consort with weaker spirits than himself.

As I intend shortly to reprint six of my papers which have daring the last two years appeared in the *Spiritualist*, I will take care to express myself so as to correct the words on which you inadvertently misinterpret my meaning.

I suppose you at once admit that the adept works chiefly in secret, and that so far he differs from those Christians who, in the history of the church, obtained divine powers. I will also note what you say about female adepts, although we in London are under the belief that H. P. B, led us to understand that no *fully* initiated female adept existed.

You say, your "fifty years" experience forces you to conclude that Christianity is a bad religion, and fosters every sin and vice against which its ethical code inveighs."

Surely you have not pondered your words — for how can a *perfect ethical code* foster every sin and vice?

What you mean is that — so-called Christian churches and priesthoods have been guilty of every sin and vice. I might with equal logic say. Buddhism must be an abominable religion, because I find the most degrading ignorance and vice is to be found in many of the lamaseries of Thibet.

But, instead of reasoning thus, I, in my address, speak of esoteric Buddhism with the greatest reverence and respect, and I assert that esoteric Christianity and esoteric Buddhism are in their central spirit identical.

I hope you may be able to insert this short letter in the *Theosophist*, because I wish my Oriental brothers to understand that, in all I write, I desire truth only, and I am prepared now and always to stand thereby at whatever cost.

Moreover, I feel this, as a conviction of my soul, that, were I admitted to intimate conversation with a truly spiritual adept, we should find our views on religion, in their central essence, identical.

Believe me, dear Brother, Yours sincerely, GEORGE WYLD, M. D.

Notes on the above

My explanations of the real motive of the Indian ascetic's severe course of self-spiritualization, as given in the article to which Dr. Wyld adverts, were so clear that, upon a second reading, I do not see that further elucidation is called for. I think I showed that the acquisition of divine powers, to use them for good of mankind and not for private benefit of any kind, was what is sought. The ascetic of India "works in secret" while developing his powers, only because contact with the *filthy selfishness* and sensualism of the world would prevent the development. And if the full adept, after becoming such, lives apart, it is because he can thus best work for humanity. Though unseen, he is nevertheless ever doing good. I recall no instances of Christian "adepts," or, indeed, any of another faith — who did not at least gain their powers by fasting, meditation, and seclusion; nor any who afterward freely lived and mingled with the gluttonous and vicious crowd. The long list of untrained religious ecstatics we will not take into account. Whether epileptics, mediums, natural clairvoyants, or mesmerized neurotics, they are not to be mentioned in the same breath with the instructed powerful initiate of Esoteric Science, to whom nature's secrets are known and her laws his auxiliaries.

I re-affirm that I have met some female ascetics possessed of magical powers, and know of more. But I did *not* say that either of these or any female had reached the highest possible degree of power in occult science; there are many stages, and all persons do not reach the same.

Dr. Wyld should not make me appear to call the Christian ethical code "perfect". If it were perfect, then it certainly would not lend itself to a double interpretation and so foster every vice and sin. In my judgement, the doctrine of vicarious atonement, the very basis of Christianity, neutralizes all its lofty moralities, since it pretends that faith, not merit, secures salvation. In this respect. Buddhism is vastly superior.

As to the degrading ignorance and vice in the lamaseries of Thibet, if Dr. Wyld has "found" them there, it must have been through the eyes of some imaginative book-maker; for no real traveller — the Abbé Huc *not* excepted — has had the chance to make such a discovery. However, let us offset the lamasery, which we do *not* know to be a nest of sensualistic recluses, against the

Christian monastery and nunnery which we *do* know to have so often been such, and confine ourselves to the main subject. The author of a very recent essay, speaking in an Australian magazine from the stand-point of personal observation says: — "On the other hand, savage and uncivilized races may be found, whose domestic life is in the highest degree moral, as the Zulus, among whom crimes, such as we reward them, do not exist, and a more honest, truthful, and chaste race is not to be found, as I can affirm from years' residence among them. And that this morality arises from intuition is proved by the fact that, when they are educated and taught 'Bible truths,' they immediately become immoral, and, like the English mistress who puts into her advertisement, 'No Irish need apply,' the Natal mistress says, 'No Christian Kuffir need apply', for, when Christianised, the men are thieves and the women unchaste."

On behalf of Buddhist, Vedaist, Jain and Parsi, I am quite satisfied to let the moral code of either of these faiths, which alike teach that merit can alone save, be compared with the code of Christianity, which teaches that the sinner may be saved from the natural consequences of his sin by faith in the vicarious efficacy of the blood of one named Jesus. As was remarked in my previous article, if my respected friend and brother. Dr. Wyld, were to study Eastern philosophies under Eastern masters, his opinions would certainly change.

H. S. OLCOTT Bombay, April 1880.

THEOSOPHY AND ITS OPPONENTS

[A Letter by Henry S. Olcott on the Hodgson Report]

Mr. Reimers has received a long and interesting letter from Colonel Olcott on the above subject, which he has handed to us for publication. In the opening sentences the Colonel expresses his pleasure at being in direct correspondence with so earnest, able, and honest a student of psychic science as Mr. Reimers, and proceeds as follows: ---

"Since my book on the Eddy mediums ('People from the Other World') appeared I have been occupying myself with the evidences for the reality of Asiatic psychic science and testing the reasonableness of the Eastern esoteric doctrine. Without going into needless particulars, I shall simply say that I have personal knowledge of (*a*) the existence of adepts with developed psychic powers of the highest order; (*b*) the existence of a complete system of spiritual philosophy transmitted from an unknown antiquity; (*c*) of there being a genuine experimental science at its basis; (*d*) of the reconciliation of the latter with our most modern scientific discoveries; (*e*) of the fact of a personal relation between the aforesaid psychic experts and Madame Blavatsky; and of her possession of certain abnormal powers covering a wide range of phenomena, from the most elementary mediumistic rappings, tiltings, and psychography up to those upon a plane where consciousness and the power of action are enjoyed extra-corporeally. To pursue my work uninterruptedly I relinquished all worldly interests in the year 1878, and since then my existence has been bound up and merged in that of the Theosophical Society. We have had stormy times, sustained many rude assaults, and suffered much cruel injustice; but the outcome of it all is that the Society has expanded beyond all expectation, has 124 branches, and this month is forming more --- among them one in Ireland and one in Africa. So whatever faults we may have made in administration, whatever offences either of us may have been charged with or committed, it is undeniable that our declared principles are good, and the platform upon which our Society stands so strong as to defy even the most violent and malevolent attacks upon personal character. As regards the recent crusade of the London S.P.R. against Madame Blavatsky, there is one thing to be said which explains why it has so little permanent effect upon our Society. The report is so full of personal pique and malice, and shows so little familiarity with psychological science, that experienced and unbiassed theosophists and spiritualists see that Mr. Hodgson has overshot his mark, and that his blow will recoil upon himself. Nothing could have been more treacherous and malicious than his attempt to give Madame Blavatsky the character of a 'Russian spy.' That theory --- as Mr. Sinnett has shown, and as official documents in my possession prove --- was abandoned within a short time after her arrival in India. Its absurdity is but too evident to every one who ever passed a fortnight in Madame B.'s company. She is the very last person in the world to whom any Government, let alone the cautious Russian, would entrust such a delicate service. But, finding absolutely no other than a philanthropic motive for her long courses of self-sacrificing devotion to theosophy, and instinctively feeling that the whole force of the crusade against her would be broken unless something wicked could be alleged against her, he deliberately revived the exploded 'spy' theory --- after arguing the pros and cons with myself and another gentleman here [at Adyar, Madras, India] and confessing its inadequacy --- backing it up with a fragment of the MSS. of an old translation she made five years ago for an Indian organ of

Government --- the *Pioneer* --- which had been pilfered and laid by with *malice prepensa* by the adorable Madame Coulomb! And he further supported it with a quotation from a sympathetic private letter from myself to a Hindu, written from New York in 1878, in the tone in which every true American would write, in answer to the patriotic plaint that the Indian princes were stripped of all their grandeur! In India the cry 'A Russian spy' has the same effect as that of "A Prussian spy' had in France of late, or that of the 'Black Horse Cavalry' had in the United States at the time of Bull Run. Mr. Hodgson knew this, and deliberately employed this convenient method of disposing of Madame B.'s case. Perhaps more than any one else here, I have been grieved and shocked with Mr. H.'s conduct, for --- as he himself admits --- I threw our most private records open to him, gave him facilities he could otherwise never had secured for investigating, and expected him to deal by us with absolute candour and loyalty. I am also sorry to be obliged to say that, for the sake of impeaching the character of Mr. Damodar --- noblest, most unselfish, and devoted of young Hindu philanthropists, and one of the most successful of our psychic experimentalists --- Mr. Hodgson suppressed an account --- capable of verification by Postal Department, and other proofs --- of an 'Astral flight,' or psychic journey, of Mr. D.'s from Cawnpore to Madras on the night of November 4, 1883, and of his transportation of a certain letter (to me from a gentleman in Italy) from Madame Blavatsky, which very letter was posted to me to Aligarh, N.W.P., on the morning of November 5, at Adyar, by Madame Blavatsky and duly reached Aligarh on the 10th, in regular course of post, where I found it on the 12th. This is so irrefutable a case, so outside of the possibility of any theory of collusion or deception, and it so upsets the plan to impeach Mr. Damodar's veracity and integrity, that it was quietly ignored. I am sorry to have to say this, but what other inference is possible when Mr. H. was shown the entries in my diary, from which he was quite willing to copy whatever suited his purpose? The same may be said respecting the evidence for Madame Blavatsky's occult powers --- whatever seemed incapable of explanation upon a gratuitous theory of fraud, falsehood, and collusion was omitted from his brief. I have no time, and it would be useless to cite the mass of facts going to prove her strange psychic endowments, as exhibited in America, Europe and Asia within the past twenty or more years; for, as regards the outside public, occult things will ever be criticised from the vulgar, material point of view, and the laws of subjective nature impertinently ignored, while the educated occultist will never allow himself to come to snap-judgments, but tests all tales of phenomena by the canons of arcane science. I recollect the case of the seizure of Mrs. Florence Corner, which you yourself witnessed, when personating a spirit at a London seance, and think it offers a very fair example in point. Undoubtedly it was she who was seized by Sir George Sitwell and Mr. von Buch, and equally certain is it that she had disrobed for the part. These sceptics, unacquainted with the laws of mediumism, were fully warranted in hastily concluding that a wilful deception was been practised by Mrs. Corner, and in so reporting to the *Times*. But, being so ignorant, it was a shame, almost a crime, that they should have assumed the role of exposers, and should have published anything whatever about the case until, by a series of seances held under scientifically perfect test conditions, they had arrived at clear proof as to the nature of the thing they were investigating. This was the course of Professor Hare, Mr. Wallace, Professor Zollner, Mr. Crookes, and other real investigators. It was also the theory upon which I worked with the Eddys, the Holmeses, and Mrs. Compton, and my over-caution as to parading my personal opinions drew from various men of science the declaration that my case was clearly proved by my facts. This instinct of caution now leads me to refrain from any *ex cathedra* declaration as to the merits of the Coulomb

Missionary Hodgson S.P.R. case against my friend and colleague Madame Blavatsky. Without omniscience nobody could penetrate to the depths of her consciousness and absolutely know whether she had tricked at all, and if so, when and how much? What we do know is that she has given numberless proofs of psychic powers, that her erudition and literary and intellectual powers are of a high order, and that for the past twelve years we have seen her labouring, like a galley slave at his oar, to spread knowledge, encourage virtuous living, present noble ideals of life for imitation, and diffuse the idea of mutual tolerance and religious comity --- and all this without asking salary, fee, or reward for herself, but, on the contrary, giving freely of her private means to help on the Society's work. Whatever her faults of character, however rough and repulsive she may seem to some, however incoherent and inconsistent others may think her, the above facts cannot be denied. And now, let such as can show a better record of useful work and unselfish life come to the tribunal and sit in judgment upon her. Temperamentally she is doubtless so organised as to constantly draw upon her own head the blows of the sceptic and the bigot; she is emphatically her own worst enemy. Moreover, she has a sort of fatal knack of doing her phenomena in a slipshod, unsystematic, and impolitic way, which too often tends to arouse suspicion in the minds of outsiders. To so old a spiritualist as you I need not say that the very same remark is to be made as regards mediums, nor that many an innocent one has been branded with imposture by hasty, self-sufficient 'investigators' --- heaven save the mark! How futile and absurd is the theory of the S.P.R. that Madame Blavatsky gradually developed the forged 'K.H.' handwriting and simultaneously eliminated her own caligraphic peculiarities; and how useless the trouble and expense they went to to prove this fact you have yourself shown in your letter under reply, where you tell me that for months you exchanged letters with an unseen intelligence, or 'spirit,' through different mediums, 'under circumstances that made the theory of trickery sheer nonsense to think of, and yet the handwriting much resembled that of the medium.' Why, it requires little more than common sense to see that this must be so, and that where a foreign influence is writing through the hand or (by precipitation) through the aura of an intermediate agent, it takes time to overcome the habitual personal peculiarities of that agent. With very negative intermediaries, of feeble will and unpronounced personality, this vicarious writing may quickly become perfected; but when the psychic agent is such a raging lion of temperament as my colleague the personal idiosyncracies must assert themselves whenever they are not quelled and made dormant by an exercise of will. With mediums, as every spiritualist knows, any temporary disturbing cause --- such as bad health or a change of health, despair about money matters, grief, violent irritation about something, fear, or any one of fifty things which affect the normal action of the brain or nervous system --- is liable to stop phenomena, or may even destroy the mediumship entirely by breaking up the passive state which had favoured its development and continuance. Even adepts recognise and conform to this law by secluding themselves from scenes and relationships which disturb the mental calm and purity of surroundings in which the psychic powers are best developed. This is the chief though not the sole reason why such men seek the solitude of the cave, the jungle, and the mountain. You have also shown me that such incidents as the apparent plagiarism of Mr. Kiddle's language in a 'K.H.' letter have no evidential value in support of a theory of conscious fraud, by citing the startling fact that in the great Handel's oratorios 'there are whole choruses, note by note, by Stradella' --- a composer who died a half-century before his time. Surely it would be an impertinent sceptic who should aver that he whom Beethoven styled the 'greatest composer that ever lived,' had consciously plagiarized from Stradella, an inferior genius! How many examples are there not of this unintentional literary appropriation not merely noted in mediumistic annals, but in those of general literature? The materialist, who has scarcely yet begun to suspect the possibility of telepathic action of thought-waves, has until now been believing that ideas, unless preserved in print or by other mechanical device, unless communicated orally to hearers of retentive memories, died away. In fact, the common proverb, *Scripta manent, verba volant* embodies this belief. As regards Mr. Hodgson's re-examination of the witnesses to appearances of the Mahatmas, all that can be said is that he has got about as near the truth as prepossessed investigators --- *e.g.* the late Dr. W. B. Carpenter and the present Dr. Lankester --- usually get in handling psychical matters. Take the testimony of witnesses to any ordinary circumstance after the lapse of two or three years --- as he did in this instance --- let alone any wonder-exciting phenomenon like the appearance of a phantom, living or dead, that was originally seen without previous expectation or prepared test conditions, and see what confusion one will get! And to think that a pretended scientific Society, with a professedly trained scientific detective, should ruthlessly traduce the characters for veracity and intelligence of as honest a body of gentlemen as can be found upon such researches as Mr. H. reports to the S.P.R. is something astonishing! Well, your spiritualism has survived nearly forty years of that sort of injustice, and perhaps theosophy will not be quite destroyed by this petard, even though its engineer may."

www.ingramcontent.com/pod-product-compliance
Lightning Source LLC
LaVergne TN
LVHW041502070426
835507LV00009B/766